A Question of Faith

Lord, You Gave Me 337.

Beverly Wickwire
Kippen Wickwire

Designed by Rob Williams
RKW Designs

To anyone who is struggling in your faith, wondering which direction God would have you take in your life, or questioning if God cares enough to answer your prayer. We pray that through the reading of these words, you will come to understand the depths of His compassion and mercy, and you will have the answers to all the questions you seek.

For my Children, who have walked with me and stood by me each step of my journey.

A Question of Faith

A few years ago, I heard a song by Steve Green called The Refiner's Fire. It was a reference to a refiner's fire which is used when extracting all the blemishes and defects from metals in order to purify them. The song talked about how as Christians, we all have to walk through life's challenges which God uses to refine our faith. I would play and sing the song when I felt like times were hard, and my spirit would be lifted.

Sometime later, God began dealing with me about writing a Bible study. When I use the phrase *dealing with me*, I mean that certain things would take place in my life, or in the life of someone I knew, that would call for an act of faith. I would give my usual spiritual response, well versed and well-practiced, and would follow that by "Eventually, I am going to write a Bible study on faith". However, the thought never went any further for me until sometime in 2002.

I can't really say the things that started taking place, but I can say God used certain and specific events to get my attention. What I did not know was that He was preparing me to walk through fire in preparation for this study.

The next few years of my life would take me into the fire, and consequently, through the fire. When I started coming out the other side, I was burned. However, this was a burn of a different kind. This was a spiritual burn, the kind that comes from the Refiner's fire that each and every Christian needs to go through at least one time in their life. It cleanses and purifies us, and it allows us to be crafted. Once we come out the other side, we are never the same.

As a result of my journey through the fire, I experienced things with God that many people dream of, but do not actually believe will ever happen to them. It is not that they do not believe God is capable, it is that they do not believe these kinds of things happen all around them each and every day.

Every time I tell my story of the events that led to this study, without fail I always get the same reactions. People want to know if these things really happened and what it was like to experience them. Then they start to make assumptions of why they would never reach this level of "spiritualism", although they would love to.

My story, told here in the following pages, is not from the life of someone we have placed high atop a spiritual plane. It is told just the way it happened, showing as has been shown so many times before, God can and will use the least of His children to accomplish His will.

This is a Bible study on faith that walks through the stages I went through as a child of God who was being taught much needed lessons in faith. As we look at my life experiences, I will parallel them with those in biblical history, and I will challenge you to examine the events of your own life.

There will likely be times you will laugh out loud as you remember your own activities, times when you softly cry as your recall personal pain, and times when you stop and stare in wonder at the thought of God's amazing faithfulness. You will see examples you never realized were there, lessons you never thought you would learn, and hope you never knew you would need. Most importantly, you will come to understand that God *IS* the Author and Sustainer of faith, and as our faith is strengthened, we will be able to walk boldly and confidently in any situation life throws at us.

As we go through this study together, I challenge you to allow your heart to be opened to the things of God and to prayerfully consider delving deeper into the doctrinal teachings of faith. If you submit to this challenge, I promise you this one thing: Your life, and the lives of those around you, will forever be changed.

Hebrews 11:1 Now faith is the substance of things hoped for, the evidence of things not seen.

James 1:5-8 If any of you lacks wisdom, let him ask of God, Who gives to all liberally and without reproach, and it will be given to him. <u>But let him ask in faith,</u> with no doubting, for he who doubts is like a wave of the sea driven and tossed by the wind. For let not that man suppose that he will receive anything from the Lord; he is a double-minded man, unstable in all his ways.

James 1:14-18 What does it profit, my brethren, if someone says he has faith but does not have works? Can faith save him? If a brother or sister is naked and destitute of daily food, and one of you says to them, "Depart in peace, be warmed and filled," but you do not give them the things which are needed for the body, what does it profit? <u>Thus also faith by itself, if it does not have works, is dead.</u> But someone will say, "You have faith, and I have works." Show me your faith without your works, and I will show you my faith by my works.

For the righteous shall live by faith

Well, if that doesn't pose immediate questions, nothing will. When I look at that statement, the first things I want to know is, am I righteous? Just exactly who is righteous? Are there lots of righteous people? Next, I want to know if the righteous are the *only ones* who live by faith. And finally, if the righteous always live by faith, then what must I do to become righteous?

Naturally, we would all like to assume we already are. After all, we are Christians and the two go hand-in-hand, right? Or do they? We also would like to assume that for the most part, we walk in faith and at the first inward glance of ourselves, I am sure it appears that we do. What happens, though, when we look deeper into our hearts and our faith is truly challenged?

I am not talking about faith in whether or not there is a God. I think it is pretty safe to assume that all of us reading this have faith that God exists. What we are talking about here is a different level of faith. This faith is much like belief in the unseen, but it is accompanied by an act, or specific actions. I like to call this **bold faith**. Let's take a look at two well-known biblical examples and how *their* lives and *our* righteousness compare.

Lesson I – The Picture of Faith – James 1:14-18 – Lord you gave me insight.

I remember the exact moment I *finally* decided it was time to write this Bible study. Oddly enough, I was sitting quietly trying not to think. My goal was to sit quietly and relax because, I was angry. The worst part was that I was angry at God.

Because of my anger, I was venting to God about the never ending saga that fueled the Refiner's fire in my life. Now, without getting into too much detail, this was one of those situations where the more I vented, the angrier I got, and the angrier I got, the more I vented. I was not crying, yelling or anything close. I had just taken a tone that was somewhat abrasive, sort of aloof, with a twist of desperation and yes, I was complaining about what I did not understand and asking what in the world I was supposed to be doing. I was also demanding to know how in the world this was supposed to benefit me.

This had gone on for a full ten minutes or so when suddenly – mid sentence – above the increasingly high volume I had achieved, I was abruptly surrounded by this statement: "Faith without works is dead." It came out of nowhere and seemingly, literally from no one. Now, you would think I would be scared to death, right? But no, not me. I was still mad. I mean, God had been allowing me to go through some terrible times and *I* was trying to be a picture of faith. So since I was not happy, the very second I heard that statement, I came back with one of my own. In a very flustered tone I replied, "Yes, God, I **know** that! You don't have to tell me that! I've been telling people that for years. So, what does that have to do with anything I am talking about?"

See what I'm saying? I was mad, and I was not about to back down. Silly me. So, here is what happened next. Without one second's hesitation, in a very sharp and much more pointed tone (that means louder, by the way), there were those words again. "Faith without works is dead!"

Notice the exclamation point? You have heard the expression "scared to death". I now know how it feels. As I sat motionless in the deafening silence, as close to death as I could feel, the next softly whispered words I heard were, "Be still and know that I AM God."

As you can imagine, I was awed and dumbfounded along with a multitude of other emotions I cannot even begin to describe. I was still. Trust me. I realized God had very sharply and clearly spoken to me, and I was in the middle of a life-altering moment.

What followed next was the epiphany. How great is that? "For I am not a God of confusion." (1 Cor. 14:33) As I stopped mouthing and sat unmoving and silent, the gentle guidance of a loving God took control of the conversation. He opened my heart and showed me that in order to walk in bold faith you must have an act of faith. There has to be an action taken, otherwise there is no basis for faith. "So, God, what You are saying is that I have to actually start writing the Bible study and trust You to fulfill Your promise, not wait

for the promise *then* be obedient to Your command."
Oh, who knew?

You see, God had called me to write this study and had promised something in return. However, in my humanity, I was expecting the promise before the act or action; sort of like having the "cart before the horse".

Finally, for the first time, I knew exactly what I had to do. So, I got myself up, prepared for the day, and without any further delay or excuse, I began writing.

Now, because of my obedience, the next few days of my life would be a nightmare. I remember coming to my poor sister-in-law, who had been placed in the position of "sounding board", and apologizing for the previous eight hours and likely the next few that were coming. I told her that like Noah and Abraham, I had to be a picture of faith if I was going to be the instrument God used to perform this particular task.

From that point on, I knew there would be continuous fights with Satan, but I knew I had God in my camp, or better yet, I was in God's camp. As I readied myself for the battles that would be bitter and heartbreaking, I placed my trust in God, knowing that He had already given me the victory.

In my study, I learned that God walks us through faith in a five step plan however, we typically follow with our own two step plan. God's plan goes like this – 1. The command/promise, 2. The preparation/action, 3. The statement/stand, 4. The completion, 5. The fulfillment. Our two step plan goes like this. 1. The command, 2. The doubt.

Ah, yes, you know the doubt. With great consistency and without missing a single step, when confronted with God's plans we react just like this. **What**?! Did that come from *God?* How do I *know* that came from God? What if that was not *really* God? Why would God want *me* to do that? What if I am *wrong*? What if I *mess* it up? What if I *cannot* do it? Get the idea? I wonder where we learned this. Is this part of the nature we are all born with, or is it something we have to learn as we grow?

I cannot say I know for sure where we get these ideas, but I can say they did not come from some of the pictures of faith God shows us in Genesis. As you read through the text, you will easily be able to see how I reached this conclusion. Take a look at what God's Word has to say on the subject of bold faith and the examples He used to show us. I am sure you recognize all these characters, and you know the stories well.

Genesis 6 – We all know this story. God told Noah to build an ark and Noah did, so he lived happily ever after. The end. How easy was that? That has to be the shortest lesson on obedience and faith we have ever heard. It is catchy and to the point. But, wait. Remember the five step plan? That plan will play out entirely in the chapters of Genesis 6 –9. When we read those chapters, we can see there was much more to this story of faith than we had previously thought. Look at the guidelines below, then take a few minutes and read the text. See if you can find these steps and how they are realized as I have them listed.

Gen 6:13-21	The Command
Gen 6:22	The Preparation
Gen 7:4	The Statement
Gen 8	The Completion
Gen 9	The Fulfillment

You see, God, in His infinite wisdom, saw that the world He created had become corrupt beyond imagination.

As a result, the Bible tells us that God was actually *sorry* He had created man. Gen., 6:5-7 paints a pretty clear picture for us. It says that God was **grieved** in His heart. What a soul searching statement. When the Bible talks here about grieving, it refers to the same sort of grief you and I experience when we lose something very close and dear to our hearts. There is emotional pain, agony, and heartbreak. This is the grief our loving God was going through, and He was grieved to the point where He no longer wanted to have man around. Thankfully for us, the story goes on in verse 8 to tell us that God did, however, find favor with one man; one man. In the midst of a corrupt and disobedient world, He was able to see the heart and life of our only hope. That man was Noah.

Because of Noah's righteousness, God decided He would not destroy the world, but instead would rebuild it through the heart and home of this one man. So without hesitation, God came to Noah and told him the plan. God said, "Noah, I'm going to destroy the earth with water, but I am going to save you. All you need to do is build this giant ark for yourself, your family, and the hundreds of species of animals I have created," (Gen. 6:14-21, paraphrased of course).

Now, remember how God works. He gave Noah a direct command and promise, and Noah reacted by following the next part of the five step plan. He simply prepared for what God said was coming. He stepped out in faith and did as he was told. He did not stand there asking all the questions of doubt we are accustomed to. Remember the ones we pointed out earlier? Instead of wasting all that time and energy, Noah trusted God and His word and moved into action. (Gen 6:22). Noah was showing his faith <u>by his works,</u>

(James 1:14-18) so, it is safe to say the *faith without works is dead* statement does not apply here. Noah built the ark exactly as specified, then made the boldest statement of all when he brought his entire family into that boat, along with all the animals commanded him, and allowed God to shut them up inside (Gen. 7:11-16). Alright, now for a deeper look.

During the events preceding the flood, there certainly was more dialogue between God and Noah than what was mentioned in the text. If that were not true, Noah would have been blindly trying to figure out how to finish the construction and get all those animals to come on board. I mean, just stop and think for a minute about if you had to board hundreds of animals. There definitely had to be lots of conversation taking place. However, there is never any mention of God speaking to any other member of Noah's family. This had to be the next step in bold faith for him.

If you think about this, Noah had to be completely trusting in God, and his family had to be completely trusting in Him. Can you imagine the head of the household trying to tell you something that would seem as ludicrous as this had to have sounded? I am sure there were moments of fear and concern from his family, but I think this is one of the reasons Noah is referred to as "righteous". His family followed him in obedience and faith, just as he followed God. Noah's family followed the value system that God had intended for the family.

As the story continues, we see that God did, in fact, bring the flood upon the earth just as He had said and, consequently, destroyed all of its inhabitants. This was the completion of the action of faith. (Gen. 7:11-24). Then came the light at the end of the tunnel, or in this particular case, the rainbow after the fulfillment of the promise.

God had issued a command and a promise, and Noah had followed in obedience and received the promise. What a beautiful story that paints a perfect picture of bold faith being carried out the way God meant for it to be. The five step plan of God followed from beginning to end.

So, what about the two step plan of man? Did you see that with Noah? Absolutely not. There was no two step plan with him. God said do it, and Noah just did it and held on to the title of "righteous". So, it is safe to say we did not learn our two step plan from Noah.

Where, then, did we come up with that idea? Maybe it was from Abraham (Abram). We all remember him. He had no history with God, and the Bible does not indicate that God had spoken to him before. Still, he was called out of nowhere to leave his family, his homeland, and his life.

He had no warning; no preparation; just a direct command from God. Let's see if he responded with the same bold faith we saw in Noah.

Genesis 12 – *"Now the Lord said to Abram, 'Go forth from your country, and from your relatives, and from your father's house, to a land which I will show you; And I will make you a great nation, and I will bless you, and make your name great; And so you shall be a blessing; And I will bless those who bless you, and the one who curses you I will curse, and in you all the families of the earth shall be blessed.'"* (Gen. 12:1-3)

The first thing we see from the start is God's command to Abram. Basically God said, "Get out", and proceeded to tell Abram how He was going to bless him. This seems to be a pattern with God. The nutshell version is that God told Abram to gather all his family and his possessions and relocate immediately. God told him to pack everything he owned; his house, his furnishings, his livestock, and his entire family and go.

So what was Abram's response? Did he stop and say, "Well now, hang on, God. Before I agree to this, where am I going? What am I going to do in this unknown place? How will I know how to get to wherever You are sending me?" No, that is not what Abram did at all. In fact, the Bible states that he simply got out. Look at verses 4 – 6. There was no hesitation, only obedience, just like we saw from Noah.

There were no moments of arguing with God. Abram exercised his faith *through* his works. (There is that lesson from James again.) He did not stop and consider a timeline or start planning his calendar and rescheduling his events. He did not concern himself with letting people know that he was not going to show up at the barbeque after church on Sunday, and he certainly did not start telling God he had to take care of these kinds of things before he could follow His command. Abram simply obeyed.

What a powerful picture of faith. Imagine packing everything you own into the back of an old pickup truck and just going until God said stop. I wonder if any of us would have that kind of bold faith and, because of that faith, take the action necessary to carry out the works portion of the lesson. Remember, <u>faith without works is dead.</u>

So there we had the command and the immediate preparation. Next came Abram's statement in verses 7 – 8. He built an altar *before* God had even fulfilled His promise. As we read the next few verses of the text, we see the obstacles Abram faced and his separation from his nephew, Lot. Here is what we do not see: The completion. Remember, when God made His promise to Noah, the fulfillment came within a few months. With Abram, it would be much different. In fact, the total fulfillment of the promise did not come until several hundred years after his death. However, as

God is always true to His promises, He did fulfill His plan, and Abram, walking in faith, trusted God's timing. So what have we learned so far?

Faith without works is dead. That is pointed out beautifully in these two examples. Both Noah and Abram were busy living their lives. Nothing special or different was going on with either of them. However, God called each of them out of the comfort zone of their lives to a place of unknown. Even so, without hesitation both of these men simply followed God's command. Think about that as you say these words out loud – *faith without works is dead*. Can you stop for just a minute and ponder that statement?

What if God had made the command, given them the promise, and their response had been, "Okay, God, I will get to that when I am sure it is time. I need to pray about it". What if they had sat and waited until they had an experience like mine. Would God have fulfilled His promise? Of course He would have, because God always holds up His end of the bargain. What we likely would have seen, though, was a *delay* in the blessings both of these men, their families, and the many generations to follow would realize. Because of the acts of the bold faith displayed by these two men, lives have been changed for centuries, and people have sought and found refuge from life's struggles through their relationship with God.

It is important for us to understand that when God called these two men into faith, in many ways it had to have been very difficult to follow the commands. Take Noah, for example. On the one hand, we like to think that if God "came to us" as He did in those days and told us to do something, it would be very easy to do. Keep in mind, though, that at this time in Noah's life, the world was not inhabited by six billion people. In fact, many scholars believe the numbers were probably much closer to the thousands.

Also remember that at that time, everyone still lived in the same general area. This was before the separation of the continents.

The Bible tells us that Noah was a "preacher of righteousness" and God gave him 120 years to build the ark. So what does all that mean? It means that Noah spent 120 years preaching to an ungodly world and, in turn, received a great deal of ridicule. Look at the facts again. There Noah was building a giant, giant boat on *dry* land. To gain even more perspective I consider the fact that the world had no perception of rain. At this time, the ground was still being watered by "the mist that came up from the earth". (Genesis 2:6) Add to that the fact the Noah was the *only* righteous man, and you can imagine the level of criticism he received. I am sure people thought he was insane building this monstrosity on land that had never seen water, while going around telling people that God was going to flood the earth and save anyone who came on board. Okay, Noah. Sure and, by the way, what is a flood? Contrast that with what happens when God asks us to share the Gospel or tell about something He has done in our lives. Even among our small knit group of friends or coworkers, we do not want to share. Notice, too, that God did not tell Noah how long He was going to give him to accomplish this task. That lets us know that since Noah was a righteous preacher of the Gospel, he was likely in panic mode as he tried to convince people to change their wicked ways. Given all these facts, we can easily see the level of faith Noah was asked to display.

We see the same story with Abram. Here is a man who was living among his family in a place where he knew everyone, and everyone knew him. As was the custom of the days, his family all lived together and helped one another. Abram was an active participant in his family and certainly would have been sorely missed when he suddenly just up and left. Can you imagine the reactions he likely received when he started packing everything he owned and told everyone who asked that he had no idea where he was going? Since we can be assured that people have not changed throughout the centuries, I am confident that Abram received more than his share of resistance and ridicule. We all know how that works in our lives. There is always someone ready to tell us what we are doing wrong and ready to laugh at us for doing what they do not agree with. This is true human nature at its finest. We can also all imagine what it must have been like when Abram broke the news to his wife, Sarai. Wouldn't you love to have been a fly on the wall for that conversation? It probably went something like this. "Hey, Hunny. How was your day? I brought you some lovely flowers. My goodness, you sure are looking particularly beautiful. Oh, by the way, today while I was working in the field, God, um, yeah, God came to me and told me to come home and pack everything we own and move. I don't know where yet, but when we get there, I will know. Now, I know this is your home and your father's house and all your friends are here, but you are just going to have to trust me. Oh, and one last thing. We have to be out by sunrise. Love ya, Hun. So anyway, when's dinner?"

I do not think I have to spend much time painting a picture of what likely happened after that. Imagine, ladies, being in the kitchen finishing up dinner when suddenly your husband bursts through the door with flowers and candy in hand and announces, "Baby, I had a talk with God today and, well, we are moving tomorrow; to a place I can't say right now because, um, I don't know where it is yet; but we'd better get started packing." Sure, I can see that one happening. Can you just see the quickness to which you would start moving in preparation to pack? Right. Maybe a quickness to find a phone and call a friend or relative to tell on him, or better yet, sic your pastor on him.

Of course, on the men's side, you can imagine, can't you, having the nerve to come through the door and fearlessly in bold faith making that huge announcement to your loving wife. I am sure right now you can get a very vivid picture of her face when you finished making those statements. Close your eyes and wait for the image. Do you see that smile and nod of affirmation? We all know the saying, "Well, that went over like a lead balloon."

Remember the way people think has never changed. We have all shared the same hopes and dreams since the beginning of time. We dream of home and family, safety and security, a place of acceptance. These are the things we believe bring peace to our lives. Kind of makes you wonder where we got the idea of peace being found in our possessions. It does not appear to have come from Abrahm.

Gen. 22 – What about peace that passes all understanding. Doesn't that come from God? Isn't He going to be the One who ushers peace into our lives? What better way of knowing and understanding peace than by carrying out an act of bold faith as God calls us into obedience?

I think probably the most perfect picture of that comes, again, from Abraham, whose name had been changed in chapter 17, along with that of his wife. Here is a man who was called away from his homeland and sent into the unknown yet, without hesitation, he willfully followed God. Years later, God blessed him with the son He had promised.

We all know the story well. God came to Sarah and Abraham when they were quite advanced in age and told them they were going to be proud parents. We also note that He came to them separately. We remember that Sarah's response was to laugh, and Abraham questioned God a bit. In the end, though, God was true to His Word and did bless their lives with a beautiful baby boy.

I am not sure if one can imagine how they must have felt, but try to put this into perspective. This was a time when a woman's importance was measured by her ability to have children, and men were considered blessed according to the number they fathered. For years, Sarah and Abraham had been unable to conceive but finally, after sixty plus years of marriage, they found themselves as parents. Imagine how they must have loved that child.

They also had the added emotions of knowing that this child would be set apart as God Himself had announced his birth. I can just bet that Sarah was the mother the word *overprotective* was modeled after. That would explain the reason that in the next act of faith God called Abraham to, we see no mention of his wife, Sarah.

The Bible tells us that after God had blessed Abraham and Sarah with this beautiful son, He told Abraham to do something that goes beyond our realm of comprehension. God told Abraham to take his only son and **sacrifice him as a burnt offering.** Okay, back up. Most of our responses would go something like this, "God, did You just say to sacrifice **MY** son as a burnt offering"? "No way! Put on the brakes, God, I need to get my ears, heart, and spirit checked because there is **NO WAY** I could, or would, ever make that kind of sacrifice! You can just forget that right now, God." Was that Abraham's response, though?

As we read Gen. 22:1-8, we find the most amazing testimony and act of faith that we will likely ever see again. The Bible tells us that Abraham was being tested by God. While we have no idea the emotions that he likely experienced, we can definitely assume. Or can we? There is never any indication that Abraham doubted God's promise for even one second. Remember, God had told him that He would give all the land to his (Abraham's) physical descendants.

God had given him the son of promise of which the descendants would be born. How then, could He possibly take away his life now? That brings new insight to verse 1 when it says that "God tested him".

I wonder if there was ever even a flicker of doubt or fear in Abraham's heart. Human nature tells us that certainly there would be, but we see no indication of that anywhere in this story. In fact, Abraham followed the five step plan, just as he had done earlier. He got his son ready, then packed all the things he would need for the trip and for the offering. The only thing missing was the actual lamb. When he reached a certain point, Abraham made his first statement of faith. He told the men who were traveling with him that he and Isaac were going up to sacrifice, and they would **both** be returning to them. (Gen. 22:5) That is bold faith. But wait. It gets way better.

The Bible tells us in Gen. 22:6-8 that as they approached the place of sacrifice, Isaac noticed they had no lamb and questioned his father about it. Look at the unwavering response of Abraham, "My son, God will provide for Himself the lamb for the burnt offering." (Gen. 22:8) Without missing a beat, they continued on until they reached their destination. Then Abraham began to do the unthinkable. He built an altar, prepared the wood, and proceeded to bound Isaac and lay him on top of the wood (Gen. 22:9). I cannot comprehend any of us being able to survive.

As you can imagine, regardless of how strong Abraham's faith was, it is important to remember that Isaac had no clue as to what was going on. After all, he was only a young boy, and there was no way he could possibly understand. It is easy to assume that Isaac had to have been scared to death and likely hysterical. This kind of emotion must have been nearly impossible for his father to handle with calmness. I can almost see Abraham weep over the fear and heartbreak of his child, just as Jesus wept (John 11:35) when Mary and Martha were so broken. But the story continues. "Abraham stretched out his hand and took the knife to slay his son." (Gen. 22:10) Certainly there had to be doubt in those flickering few seconds of time as Abraham fully and completely followed God's command.

Try to place yourself in this moment. Picture the horror in Isaac's eyes and the panic in his motions. It rips at my heart to think of the tears that would be flooding Abraham's face as he gave himself over to the will of God. What an incredible few seconds this had to have been. No words could cover the emotions that would have been playing out. Then, as is always the case, God came through and fulfilled His promise. Look what happened next.

"But the *Angel of the Lord* (Jesus) called to him from heaven and said, 'Abraham. Abraham!' so he said, 'Here I am.' And He said, 'Do not lay your hand on the lad, or do anything to him, for now I know that you fear God, since you have not withheld your son, your only son, from Me.'" (Gen. 22:11-12).

What an intense moment in time. That few seconds had to have seemed like an eternity to Abraham. I cannot begin to imagine the strength and faith it took to follow God and to trust Him all the way to that point. God immediately told Abraham He was pleased with him and, as promised, delivered to him the animal for sacrifice (Gen. 22:13).

Go back with me for a moment to verse 8 and these powerful words by Abraham: "God will provide for Himself the lamb." Abraham never moved. He stayed grounded in his faith through the entire gut-wrenching experience. Reflect on this story and imagine yourself in Abraham's and Isaac's shoes. Think of someone you love more than anything in life. Once you have that person in mind, think of some fond memories you have of spending time with them, and ponder that for a few seconds. Now, try to imagine having to give them up to God in the same way Abraham was asked to, and to trust God wholly and completely as you move to accomplish His will.

I am not convinced that any of us could be this strong. This is why I believe this to be the most beautiful picture of bold faith that has ever been portrayed.

I wonder what the world would be like if we could all exemplify the same kind of strength in our faith. God wants us all to walk in faith, but it takes strength in our character to do so. It is important for us to keep in mind, though, that we are not born with a great character. We are all born into sin and with a sin nature. If we want to grow in our faith, we have to grow in our character. That is accomplished through our relationship with God; through prayer and the study of His word.

We have looked at two of the strongest characters of bold faith in the Bible. Hopefully, we have gained insight into what it takes to achieve that same faith in our own lives. At some point, we will all be challenged and asked to walk in bold faith. Maybe when it happens, we can look to these two men and remind ourselves, "Faith without works is dead." God presents the task. We respond by taking the action. Then, the promise is fulfilled.

Lesson II – The Power of Faith – James 1:5-8 – Lord, You gave me 337.

Throughout my life, I have been called into situations where I would be forced (or allowed) to walk in faith. Sometimes, I would find myself walking boldly and in complete confidence of what God was going to do, while other times, I would be barely crawling and hoping for the best in the end. I am not sure what it was that made some of the challenges different. It certainly was not the level of difficulty that God would have to overcome in order to accomplish His plan. There is nothing too difficult for Him. Clearly, the problem was with me. James tells us very plainly in his epistle that we are to come to God asking anything of Him, and He will give it to us.

However, we are to come to Him **without doubt.** Ah, doubt. There is that word again. You have to wonder how that keeps creeping up on us. I especially have to ask myself that question when God has been so willing over and over in my life to give me exactly what I asked for. It would take me pages and pages to tell the things He has done in my life that I firmly believe were a result of my asking. Jesus said, "You have not because you ask not." That is a powerful statement. He follows that with "Ask anything in My name, and it will be given to you." Now, these are very direct and very clear statements made by God. Keep in mind, this is not some friend or family member making us a promise. This is God. **God** said, "You have not because you ask not." He did not say we have not because He is not capable of giving, or He does not want to. He says it is our fault.

Wow, that sheds a new light on things. For many years, people have asked me how it is that God always answers my prayers, and my response is always the same. God answers everyone's prayers. Sometimes, we just do not recognize the answers. Sometimes, we give up and by the time He does answer, we do not recognize the fact. The Bible teaches us that our answers lie in our specific prayer, therefore when I pray, I do not use generalities. The Bible also teaches that when we place our hope in God, He changes our desires. I think it is important that as we look at "ask anything and you will receive", we look quickly at Ps 37:4. "Delight in the Lord, and He will give you the desires of your heart." What is this saying? If we find our happiness in God, He will give us whatever we want? Hardly. There are many people who are at peace with God but do not always receive the things they ask for. So what is the Text saying to us? We have to look at the original translation to get a clearer understanding, but the key word in this verse is delight. The word here means the same things as "to put your hopes and dreams in;" "find peace and joy in." It is important for us to remember such things as, "The effective prayer of a righteous man accomplishes much," (James 5:16). Remember, "God hears the prayers of the righteous." (Prov. 15:29)

So what happens to makes us righteous? We trust God, put our faith in Him, develop a relationship with Him, walk in His ways, and allow Him to transform us. Once we are transformed, we have a new thought process. Our hearts become like His heart, and we want the same things He wants. With that new insight, we can reread the Text. "Delight in the Lord, and He will give you the desires of your heart." Once we make that transformation, our hearts are like His. Then, His desires become our desires, and when we come before Him and ask for something, He is happy to give it to us because, we are of the same mind. Remember now, we are addressing the issue of "you have not because you ask not," and "ask anything in My name and it will be given to you."

Recently, I was placed in a situation where my faith would be challenged and stretched further than I thought I would be able to handle. I had fallen hopelessly in love with a wonderful man, but our relationship faced many challenges. We met while he was home on leave from serving our country in Iraq. When he returned to duty, we made promises we both fully intended to keep. However, because of a misunderstanding, our relationship would become the tool that would be used to shovel me back into the

Refiner's fire. When he finally came home, we began trying to build our relationship but were met by so many problems, it seemed a constant battle.

After two months of trying to work through the hurdles, things ended abruptly. My heart was broken, and I was sure I would never be able to recover. I think most everyone has experienced this kind of pain at some time in their life. To me, it felt like a death, but I was quick to thank God that this man was alive and well, even though we were apart.

As days turned into weeks, the promises of "it will get better with time," became words that I no longer could believe. I spent my days thinking about him and praying for him and our relationship in general. I would cry, pray, and beg God that I would hear from him, even if it was negative. Weeks went by and I heard nothing. I thought I was not going to survive.

Then one morning while driving to work, I started praying. While this was not an uncommon practice for me, the way I prayed that morning was somehow different. I remember it was pouring rain, and the day seemed so dark. I cried out and told God that I could not bear this any longer. I did not know what I needed to say or ask, but I knew that I had to lay myself before God in order to move forward in my life. I told Him that I needed to know if this man and I were going to be together, or if I needed help to get over him. But, how would I find this out? After all, I had been begging God to help me for months.

Suddenly, it came to me. A flicker of hope; a way to move on. I knew what to do. I asked God for a specific sign, just as I had done so many times in my past. What had taken me so long is a complete mystery to me to this day. In my desperation, I told God that I needed for Him to show me the numbers **337**. I know this sounds very strange, but the story gets better. I continued on and told God that I did not care where it was, or what form it was in, but if He would show me this specific number, I would know this man and I would eventually be together and everything would be fine.

At the time of this prayer, I was driving down a long, dreary highway in the middle of nowhere. I assessed the situation then promptly said to God, "Father, I am in the middle of nowhere, and I know there is no way there is going to be a 337 on anything around here. Still, if You will show it to me, I will know, and *I will walk in faith* that You gave it to me."

I went on and told God that if I did not see that sign, I would go home after work and write a good-bye letter to this man, with a promise of moving on with my life. At that, I stopped crying and began looking diligently for the number. A few seconds later, I added a side note for God. I told Him that in order for me to know this was really from Him, I would have to see this sign before I reached my destination.

Now, let me set the scene. I was driving on a highway that ran through the middle of the country. You know the place. Random houses, occasional corner stores, cows. Yeah, that kind of country. The distance from the time I started praying until I would reach my destination was around twenty miles, so I was literally looking at twenty miles of random houses and cows. The situation seemed very bleak, and the longer I drove, the more the fear was building.

As I neared the very last turn, I began to feel myself start to panic. I had looked everywhere I possibly could to find that number. The closer I got to the end of the road, the more horrified and dismayed I became. Now I found myself wishing I had not asked this of God as it became painstakingly obvious that I was going to have to give up on my dream. I turned onto the street of my destination and finally surrendered to the reality that God was not going to show me my sign, and my relationship was permanently over. Overcome with emotion, I began to sob uncontrollably while thanking God for hearing my prayer and telling Him I would go home and write that letter.

I had resolved the situation by laying it before Christ and though I was heartbroken, I knew what I was going to have to do. I stopped crying and began wiping the tears from my face just in time to look over and see a white mailbox with beautiful flowers all around the base. As I passed, I spoke these words out loud. "That is not what I just saw." I stopped the car in the middle of the street, put it in reverse and went back for a second look. Instantly, I was back to tears as I stared in amazement at the very large **3 3 7** posted there on that mailbox. I was less than 100 feet from my destination. There are no words that could describe all I felt, and there was nothing but silence. A huge part of me wanted to get out of the car and lay face down in the middle of the street and praise God. Had it not been for the heavy rain, I likely would have done exactly that. Instead, I praised Him from the inside of the car. From that moment on, I knew my life could never be the same. I adapted this phrase which I have spoken to Him so many, many times since that day, "Lord, You gave me 337."

As the study continues, I challenge you to find your own specific sign that God can use to carry you through the toughest moments in your life. Throughout the lessons, we will go back to this over and over again. I will also share many of the times prior to this when God came through because I prayed directly and specifically. Before we continue in this journey, take a moment and ask God to open your heart and mind in order that you will see and believe the things He reveals to you.

As before, let's look to the Bible for confirmation of this faith. We will start with Abraham, who we left off with previously. From there, we will move on to the story of Abraham's servant, then to Shadrach, Meshach, and Abed-Nego, as well as Hannah. We will end with the story of Gideon. As we read and study, we will see where we find our basis for specific prayer and the unique opportunities for witness that are opened to us when we walk in this faith. Our first lesson was on bold faith. This one will focus on **blind faith.**

Gen. 24 – As we look at the next characters in our study, we see something a little different from our previous examples. This difference does not come in their level of faith, however. Instead, it comes in the steps of faith. Notice when we studied about bold faith, we said that God always uses a five step plan to accomplish His purpose. Though there is still a plan, the steps are a little different when we are walking in blind faith. This is the kind of faith where rather than God coming to us and telling us a specific action to take, we come to Him and ask Him to give us a specific action to follow. Though it seems reversed, this is the same thinking that I followed with my 337.

I wonder who thought of that first. I cannot say for sure who actually did, but I know the first notation is found in Genesis 24. As the chapter begins, we find a conversation taking place between Abraham and " . . . the oldest servant of his house who ruled over all he had," (Gen. 24:2). The Bible tells us there in the first few verses that Abraham was old and knew his life was coming to an end. As with any parent, his first concern was with his son. Some things never change, do they?

As we read through the verse, we see that Abraham told his servant to go to his homeland and find a wife for his son, Isaac. The servant was concerned about what to do if she would not come with him, so Abraham gave him an out, just in case. Genesis 24:10 begins to tell the first story of blind faith we find in the Bible as this servant calls out to God for a specific sign. Ahh, could this be **his** 337? Maybe; maybe not; but certainly something like it. Look what he asked for. Here in 24:12 he prays, "O, Lord ***God of my master Abraham***," then in 13 he continues, "behold, here I stand by the well of water, and the daughters of the men of the city are coming out to draw water. *Now let it be that the young woman to whom I say, 'please let down your pitcher that I may drink' and she says 'drink, and I will also give your camels a drink', let her be the one You have appointed for Your servant*

Isaac. And by this I will know that You have shown kindness to my master."

Do you see what just happened? This servant, who had obviously learned faith from Abraham's example, was now practicing faith of his own accord. He asked God to show him, without question, who the woman was for Isaac. In this case, he did not want to disappoint his master, Abraham, so he relied on God to show him how to carry out the task Abraham had placed before him. Notice, the Bible never says that he stopped and wondered what would happen if no woman showed up and said those words. Interesting, wouldn't you say? This servant simply laid out the plan, then proceeded to follow it. He knew that God was able to give him what he was asking, and he trusted God to give it to him.

As the story continues, we see in 24:15 that before he even finished speaking, Rebekah came out carrying her pitcher. As we read on through verse 22, the story unfolds just as he had asked. Remember James 1:5-8? This is the scripture that tells us to pray without doubting, for if we doubt, our prayer is considered useless. Now, there is a powerful statement.

So what God is saying is, when you pray with blind faith, you come before Him believing and expecting Him to give you what you are asking. Again, let's go back to Jesus' words where He tells us ". . . ask anything in My name, and it will be given to you," (John 14:14). Those are direct words from the Lord Himself as are, "You have not because you ask not," (James 4:2). God is telling us and showing us how to get the things that are important in life. When our hearts are changed, the important things in our life are made to be the same as the important things to God. When we walk with Him and look to Him for answers, He gives them to us.

What if this servant of Abraham had wavered in his faith? Would God's plan for Isaac and Rebekah to be married have fallen into place? Of course it would have because remember, God's plan always plays out the way He intends. So, if His plan is going to go on regardless of our actions, what is the point? Could it be to show people that He cares enough to hear his children, and that He cares enough to take the time to answer a prayer that matters to one person? What an awesome and eye opening thought. But just think for a moment.

Had this servant doubted God would answer him, he would have certainly missed the blessing of seeing God come through and answer his prayer. It is also important to note that though God's will can be, and will always be, carried out, He allows us to be participants in completing the plan. There is something to reflect on. God does not *need* our help.

He never has, and He never will. He simply allows us the excitement of being a part of making something happen. This is much like when we allow our own children to "help" us with a task. As they eagerly assist us in any way we ask, their hearts are filled with pride and the feeling of being needed. They receive a blessing and "pat on the back" from us, and this brings them great joy. Back in verses 29-67, we see that the servant goes on and tells his story to Rebekah then afterwards, proceeds to tell it again to her entire family.

Look at the awesome effect and opportunity for witnessing. First, the servant got to experience his own personal encounter with God. Next, he shared with Rebekah and allowed her to be part of, and to share in, the experience. Then, he told a countless number in her family who, no doubt, told other members of the community. How amazing is that? So what we see is a prayer spoken in faith, a prayer immediately answered, then a sharing of the story for the purpose of strengthening faith. Now *that's* how it is supposed to be done. God gives us the miracles of faith, and we are to share them with the world so that faith can grow.

Through the years, I have told countless stories of things God has done – prayers He has answered – that only mattered to me or me and my family. It's so funny. I was always quick to thank God because I would know these events would be a direct result of my prayer, but I would also be amazed that He answered. I have no idea why. I remember the time we were struggling financially in our lives and had an electric bill due by the end of the day. I had absolutely exhausted every avenue to come up with the money to pay it. I had even gone to the church, but nothing worked out. So *after* I tried everything humanly possible, I decided to give the problem to God. Funny how that works. I came before Him in tears and told Him that He was my last hope and that if He did not come through, my family would have no electricity the next day. Do you wonder why I did not make Him my only hope? I know I do, but anyway, I finished my prayer, got up off my knees (yes, it was that kind of prayer), wiped my face and went on with my day.

Around 3 p.m., I went out to get the mail. I was as disgusted as I pitched each piece onto the counter. Bill, another bill, another bill, junk mail from the mortgage company, more bills. I opened them and put them away in their appropriate file and started to throw out the three pieces of junk mail when something told me, "Open the piece from the mortgage company." As I opened it, I looked through several pages of gibberish about our mortgage, then at the very bottom of the last page there was a check for overpayment of escrow. Now I want you to understand that the electric bill was $348.27. I was completely overwhelmed as I looked at the check for $348.73. I laughed; I shouted; I cried; I called out to my children. I got on the phone and started telling people and, you know what? The only ones who were really excited were me and my children. Everyone else listened and all were happy for me, but we (my children and I) were *changed*.

To this day, I marvel in this one of many stories and to this day, I have no idea why God gave us the extra 46 cents. Who knows, maybe someday we will understand. Maybe not. What I do know is this. God loves me and cares enough to hear me, even when I put Him last. I can only hope that someday I will be able to reach the level of understanding and trust that reminds me to call on God first and walk in the assurance that He will come through and take care of me. Let's look on to our next characters.

Dan. 3 – We all know the great story of Shadrach, Meshach and Abed-nego, right? They were those guys who were thrown into the fiery furnace and God kept them safe. This is truly a great story and I suspect, when you ask most people, that would be the extent of their knowledge of this story from beginning to end. However, there has to be more to it than that. After all, a story cannot possibly become this well known if it is that simple, can it?

As we start reading the book of Daniel, chapter 3, we find that King Nebuchadnezzar is in power and is out of God's will. In the previous two chapters, we were told that he had been having dreams that kept him in constant turmoil, so he had called on the wise men of his kingdom to reveal the meaning of these dreams. In accordance with God's plan, these wise men were unable to interpret the meanings, so the king had Daniel bought to him, having heard that he could achieve the task. As the story continues, Daniel makes the interpretations (Dan 2:47), and we see Nebuchadnezzar humbly confess that Daniel's God is, in fact, **THE** God.

You would think after such a confession, Nebuchadnezzar's life would take on a permanent change for the better. However, this does not prove to be the case. Though he had been privy to the revelation of **Who** God Is, the king still returned to his old ways, including idol worship. As a result, he had a ninety foot image of gold made, and it was erected in the middle of the plains (3:1). If that was not bad enough, he then ordered that all the people of the kingdom had to stop, bow down, and worship this image when they heard certain instruments playing. Of course, there would be punishment of death for anyone who defied the king's command, and in keeping with all prior payments for disobedience, it would be a horrific death. In this case, the death would come by being cast into a fiery furnace so that the offenders would be burned alive (Dan. 3:2-7). Kind of graphic, wouldn't you say? You do have to admit, though, the plan was effective. Almost every single person in the kingdom would find themselves on their face the second they heard those instruments. This is where the story turns to the faith of three young men.

If you know the story, you will remember that Shadrach, Meshach, and Abed-Nego were only in Babylon because they had been captured and forced to serve the king. They performed the daily duties required of them in order to be in compliance with their job. However, when it came to the object of their worship, this would be a completely different circumstance. These three young men made the bold decision they would not bow down and worship this image, no matter what the cost. What a scary time this had to have been for these guys. They had to have known that it would only be a matter of time before they were reported and, sure enough, that is exactly what happened (Dan. 3:8-10).

In the next few verses (Dan. 3:14-18), the exchange between the king and these three men is recorded. King Nebuchadnezzar gave them an opportunity to "redeem themselves" or put their faith to the test. The Bible tells us that he told them they would be cast into the furnace if they did not comply. Then the king asked a very pointed question that tests the very realms of comprehension considering all he had learned about

God. Nebuchadnezzar asked them "Who is the God Who would deliver you from 'my' hand," (Dan. 3:15)? Oh . . . my. I can almost see the look of mockery on his face. But, here is a better question. Who, in their right mind, would dare to put God to the test? Well, I guess no one said that the king was sane.

The next thing we see is the beautiful response and statement of faith given by these young men. Look at what they said and the assurance and boldness with which they spoke. "O, Nebuchadnezzar, we have no need to answer you in this matter. If that is the case, our God Whom we serve IS able to deliver us from the burning fiery furnace, and He will deliver us from *your* hand, O king," (Dan. 3:16-17). Wow! What great strength that took.

Picture yourself standing before the king who has the power to execute you at any second. Now, picture yourself telling him face to face that you will not do as he commands. Not only that, but for him to do whatever he wants to you because you know, for a fact, that God will save you from anything he (the king) does. If that is not a statement of faith, there is none to be found. This is blind faith in its most vivid form. God had not told them as He had told Noah and Abraham to do this specific thing. They simply *knew* God's heart and spoke based on that knowledge. What if we all knew God's heart in that way? Could we, or would we, be willing to trust Him to that extent?

As the story continues we see that the king was infuriated and had them bound and cast into the furnace, just as he had promised. But that was not good enough for him. To add fuel to the fire, no pun intended, he had the furnace heated up by seven times. The Bible tells us it was so hot that the men who cast our three young heroes inside were immediately incinerated (Dan. 3:19-22). What happened next is what I like to call "so God".

The next morning, the king went to look inside the furnace fully expecting to find no one alive. What he saw instead was not only our three heroes of faith but, much to his amazement, there was a fourth man. According to the king's own words, this man was ". . . like the Son of God," (Dan. 3:25). He questioned his counselors and said, "Wait, guys, didn't we throw three men in here," (Verses 24-25, paraphrased)?

Then came the pay-off for the courageous statement of faith made by these three amazing men of God. The king went before the opening of the furnace and called out to them by name, then referred to them as 'servants of the Most High God'. As they immerged from the fire and smoke, there is no doubt as to the incredible humbling felt by the king. He and his counselors took note of the fact that nothing was burned or singed on them, nor did they even smell as though they had been near a fire. There is also no mention of the fourth man coming out with them or of any body being recovered.

After that, Nebuchadnezzar remembered the power of God and, finally, gave Him the praise He deserved. Then, he ordered that if anyone spoke a word against God, the punishment would be harsh (Dan. 3:28-29). As a reward, the king promoted these young men to oversee his province.

When we look at the whole story, we see there was much more to it than these young men being saved from a fiery furnace. What we find is the faith of three young men, their strength as they faced incredible circumstances, and deliverance by God, Who is the only One able to save.

I wonder what it was like to be walking in that furnace with the Angel of the Lord; our God there with them; to have an entire evening in the presence of Him. I wonder if any of us would be willing to face a fiery furnace in order to have that same type of experience.

As a result of the faith of these young men, Nebuchadnezzar was given a second chance to come to God in faith. He was humbled before God and men and was made to confess that God is the only God. But remember, life changing faith leads to life changing faith. Consider the number of people whose lives were forever changed after these events. The numbers are endless. Let's continue with our next example.

How many times have we said to God, "Lord, if You will just give me 'this', I will do 'that' for You in exchange?" If we could pile up a dollar for every time someone said that, there would be no shortage of money anywhere in the world. However, what generally happens is, we come to God in a moment of emotion and beg Him for something we may or may not need, then immediately go on with our lives as though nothing has happened.

First of all, when we ask for something, we do not need to promise God something in return. Here are some examples. "God, if You will just give me that great job, I will give You the tithe before I spend anything else." Or, "God if You will help me pass this test, I will help someone else who does not understand." "If You will heal this person, I will tell everyone about You and all the things You have done for me in my life."

How about this? What if we did all the things God asked us to do without trying to use them as a bargaining chip to get Him to give us things we want in life? If we do choose to try and bargain with God, we better be willing to hold up our end of the bargain.

Think about those times when God has done what we ask of Him. How do we respond?

I remember after God gave me my very first 337. I rejoiced in that moment and walked on clouds for days. But, as is usually the case, I soon began to lose that momentum. I learned something about myself that I had never noticed. I found that in my life, I am able to maintain hope for about three or four days. After that, I begin to fall victim to the lies of Satan.

Though God had answered my prayer and given me exactly what I asked, as days turned into weeks with no contact from the man I loved, I found myself gradually spiraling back own into the pit that would leave me hopeless, angry, insecure and alone. Once I reached the bottom of the pit, I was back on my face before God begging Him to show me, once again, my 337. I remember it well. I had been telling everyone who would listen what God had done and what He was still going to do. But as days passed and my spirit dwindled, I told less and less people. When Satan finally had me almost at the bottom, I was dealt what I thought to be his final devastating blow.

In the middle of the evening, I received a phone call from an unknown woman that confirmed my worst fears about my relationship. Though the conversation was very brief, it left me an emotional wreck. That entire night, I was unable to sleep and the next day, I poured every emotion I had into a very scathing email which I sent it to this love of my life. I lost sight of hope, and I lost an entire day that I can never get back. I remember telling God over and over that it was not Him I was losing faith in, it was myself. What if I had prayed something wrong, or done something wrong, or if He had misunderstood something I had said. What if, what if, what if?

What happened to my promise of walking in faith? Where was all the elation and eagerness to praise God I had that day in the rain? How could I have possibly given in to the lies of Satan after God had been so faithful? After an entire day of wallowing, crying, and praying, in utter exhaustion I came before God and repented. I begged Him to forgive me for my lack of faith and asked Him to strengthen me. I could not believe I had let Satan get me down so far, but I had. For that, as well as every entrusting action of the day, I was truly sorry.

After I repented, I could feel the calming spirit of God all around me, and I was ready to get on with what was left of my day. I told God I was going downstairs to get back to my Bible study on Joshua. Emotionally drained, I walked down the stairs, picked up my Bible, and flipped it open. In amazement, I stared as it opened up to page 337. I was silent and motionless for about a second. Then, overcome by emotion, I thanked God for His promise and for giving this to me at a time when He knew I so desperately needed it. Once I was able to get past the tears, I turned back and saw these words. "For I am not a God of confusion," (1 Cor. 14:33). I begged God again to forgive me for my doubt and assured Him, once more, that it was me I had lost faith in, not Him. The emotions of the moment allowed me to hear the words of a song which God led me to write. It was through the song that I would be able to find comfort and peace when I was battling Satan and his lies. God was there all along, faithful to His promise. I was the one who kept doubting. Still, in His compassion, He saw fit to pick me up, forgive me, and gently put me back on the path.

Take a moment to reflect on what an awesome and amazingly gracious Father we serve and thank Him for the things He has done, and is yet to do, in your life.

<u>1 Samuel 1:1-2:21</u> – In the opening pages of 1 Samuel, we find the story of Hannah, and we see the passion of her prayers. The story opens in verses 1-7 telling about Elkanah and his two wives, Peninnah and Hannah. As we read, we find that Peninnah had been able to give children to her husband while Hannah was barren. It is important to remember that, as with Abraham and Sarah, this was a time when a woman's worth was measured by her ability to produce the offspring of her husband. The Bible tells us that Hannah was devastated by her inability and, to rub salt into the wound, Peninnah would continuously taunt her. How childish

this seems to us, but that was very common during this era. Elkanah was distressed because of his wife's pain and tried to cheer her up but, regardless of how much he loved her, she was still unhappy. Having had enough, Hannah came before the Lord and begged Him for a child. She made a vow that if He would bless her with a male child, she would give the child back to Him and a razor would never touch his head (Verse 11). Now, Eli, the priest, was sitting there watching as Hannah silently prayed. When she became emotional, he assumed that she was drunk and rebuked her. Hannah being a woman with a gentle spirit, very quietly explained to Eli what she was actually doing and convinced him that she was not drunk.

In desperation, Hannah had done the only thing she knew to do. She had come before her God, in faith, knowing that He was her only hope for a child. In return, she would be faithful to her word. Hannah had made the kind of deal with God that so many of us still try to make. Remember how it goes? "God, if you will do this for me . . .". The difference is that Hannah got up from her knees believing God had heard her and when she left that place, she had a new attitude.

As she turned to leave, Eli, clearly having heard from God, told her to go in peace for God was going to give her what she asked for (Verses 12-17). Now, Hannah had a choice to make. She could either have complete and total faith in God, or she could "hope" He would answer her. For her, the choice was simple. She was a woman of faith who had put her trust in God. Therefore, she would choose to believe that He would give her what she had asked for, and she would walk away from there with her head held high.

I wonder how many of us could have come before God and asked Him for something of this magnitude. Let your mind grasp this for a moment. All she had ever wanted in this world was to have a child, yet she promised God that if He would give her a son, she would give him back for service to God. What an incredible act that had to have been. Yet, that is exactly what she did. As the story continues, we read about the birth of Samuel and how Hannah kept her end of the bargain without hesitation (Verses 18-28).

Let's all examine our hearts for a moment. How many times have we promised God something then, when the time came for us to deliver, we backed down? In my own life, I cannot even count how many times that has happened to me. At the time I make the promise, I fully intend to keep it. However, when the time comes for me to follow through, I fall short. Even after His faithfulness with my 337, I would find myself failing. Remember, all I was supposed to do was *believe* Him, and though I truly did believe **Him,** I found myself wrestling with doubts of myself. Thankfully, this did not happen with Hannah. What would have happened had she not followed through with her promise? Remember, Samuel went on to be the last judge of Israel and the first prophet in time. He was the one God would use to guide Saul through his reign as king, and he would later anoint David as successor to the throne.

If Hannah had failed to keep her word, would God have had His way? Of course, He would have. We have said this many times throughout this study. What happens, though, when we are disobedient? We rob ourselves and countless others of the blessings we were going to receive. Generally, these are blessings that help us to walk in our faith, and they are stories that are passed on time and time again in order to help others walk and grow in faith. Think about that the next time you come before God and make a "deal" with Him. Remember, God will be faithful to keep His end of the bargain. The question is, will your faith be strong enough for you to hold up yours?

As I found myself buried in the writing of this Bible study, every day would present itself with new tests of faith, new pitfalls, and new challenges. Though I knew God had spoken plainly and deliberately when He told me to get started writing, there were many times I would be filled with fears and doubts. Now what do we know about these two emotions? We know they do not come from God. "For I have not given you a spirit of timidity but one of power, love, and self-discipline," (II Timothy 1:7). That is pretty plain as far as I am concerned.

So, if they don't come from God, where do they come from? They come from Satan. When God tells us to do something, what is the best trick Satan can use to prevent us from carrying out the task? He can simply attack our confidence. This lack of confidence manifests itself in fear and doubt and, ultimately, leaves us with a choice to sink or swim.

Though we did not talk about him in this study, we saw the same thing happen with Moses. Remember in Exodus 3 when God told Moses that He wanted him to go to Pharaoh and tell him to let His people go. He was also told to go to His people and tell them God was going to deliver them. If you have not read Exodus 3, take a few minutes and read it before you continue.

Now get the picture here. Moses was just hanging out by the mountain and suddenly this bush began burning, but not burning up. Okay. Stop here and rewind. No fire around; no one smoking; no lightning storm. Just whoosh. Fire! I can see Moses looking around with that half fear-half amazed look as he fought off the urge to run away. Then suddenly, in the midst of the fire, was the Angel of the Lord. I cannot begin to imagine what was going through Moses' head, but before he could figure it out, the voice of God came from the bush. We all know the story. In Exodus 3:7, God began to tell Moses what He wanted from him, and Moses put up one excuse after another. I do not know about you, but I would like to think that if God appeared to me in flames and said "go do anything", there would be no argument on my part. But, who knows. I am the one who God gave the 337 to, and I repeatedly doubt myself. That disqualifies me as anyone who could make that call.

We also have to keep in mind that this was Moses' first encounter with God. Remember, Moses was born from a Hebrew family but had been raised in the palace as an Egyptian. All he had ever been taught was the different forms of idol worship, and he had been led to believe that the God of the Hebrews was nothing compared to the many gods of the Egyptians.

I am fascinated by the fact that Moses did not turn and run and soon as he saw the fire. Not only did he stay to investigate what was going on with the bush, he also stuck around after the voice of God (Whom he had never known) began speaking to him. At any given time, he could have rejected everything he was witnessing and left that mountain. However, something within his being kept him there. Maybe it was the desire that God places in all men to know their Creator. No one will ever know for sure, but we can all make assumptions based on how we would have likely reacted. Regardless, the end result is the same, just as God knew it would be.

As the story goes on, we find that Moses puts up every excuse imaginable, and God has a perfect response to each one. That is the way God works. When He calls you to perform a task, He always gives you the tools necessary to complete it. The one thing He does not give us is faith. That has to come from within ourselves. Moses had to find that within even his own heart. After that, he would begin a journey that would change history and fulfill the promise God had made to Abraham over 400 years earlier. Thank God for Moses' faith and obedience.

Judges 6-8 – One of the things you can always say about God is that He is consistent in the way He does things. If you ever have any doubt, just look to the Scriptures. You remember the Old Testament stories. During and even after the Exodus, the children of Israel would fall back into their same patterns of wickedness. They would get themselves into trouble, cry out to God, and He would deliver them. This would happen over and over again. What a picture of grace and forgiveness we find in these texts. Such was the case when God called Gideon to do what seemed to be an impossible task.

Once again, the children of Israel found themselves oppressed by an evil nation, so they cried out to God for deliverance. As with all the other times, God heard their cries and sent a prophet to tell them that He had. So, we see in Jud. 6:11-13 that the Angel of the Lord appeared to Gideon while he was working in the field. In fact, the Bible tells us ". . . the Angel of the Lord came and sat under the oak . . . and said to him, 'The Lord is with you, O valiant warrior'."

Look at the interesting response of Gideon. There he is in the field working when God appears and starts speaking with him. I do not know about you, but my response would have been to hit the dirt, half out of fear and half out of awe, and probably stay there for a long time. But not Gideon. He was having a pity party, much like mine, and just like me, he was a little irritated. So what did he do? The obvious, of course. Gideon stood up and promptly said, "Well, if that is the case, then WHY has all this bad stuff happened? Where are all the things YOU promised, and HOW did we end up here?" This, of course, is a paraphrase of Jud. 6:13, but that is so like us, isn't it? God shows us every day that He is with us, and we balk at Him.

I can just see the anger in Gideon's face as he shakes his fist at God. At any given time, God could have just squashed him like a bug. But God, in His infinite wisdom and patience, simply told Gideon that He was sending him to save Israel from the Midianites (Verse 14). How funny. Now, let me just take a moment to defend Gideon the way I did Moses. When the Angel of the Lord first appeared to Gideon, he had no idea Who he was talking to. Notice that God did not tell Gideon that He was the Lord God until *after* they had been speaking for a few minutes. In fact, it seems that it was not until verse 14 that God sort of jokingly told Gideon and hinted that He was, in fact, God. Look at it. "Then the Lord turned to him and said, "Go in this might of yours, and you shall save Israel from the hand of the Midianites. Have *I* not sent you'?"

Do you hear the tone? Obviously, Gideon's lack of fear was what caused God to choose him for this huge task. So Gideon, now face to face with the Angel of the Lord, *thought* it might be God but needed to be absolutely certain before he took on the job. We cannot really blame Gideon for that, can we?

So he asked God for a sign to prove it was, in fact, Him that he was speaking with. The Lord, again showing His patience and grace, proceeded to prove Himself to the young Gideon (Verses 15-24). After that, Gideon knew for sure He was being called by God to walk in faith and take an action, and he had a new attitude. Of course, Satan was not going to sit idly by and just let that happen so, just as we would expect, the fear and doubt crept in. As a result of Satan's meddling, we see Gideon tell God that if He is actually going to save Israel through him, he was going to need another sign to prove it. After all, what if he had misunderstood God? Boy, this sounds familiar. Gideon needed his 337. I know what that is like. Chances are, so do you.

So this is when he went on to tell God that he would lay out a fleece, and when the morning came, if the fleece was wet with dew but the ground was dry, he would *know for sure this time* that it was going to be as God had said (Verses 36-37). How many times is that for Gideon now?

As we all know, the fleece was soaked the next morning and the ground was dry (verse 38), so Gideon went out and saved Israel, just like he said, right? Well of course he did not. It was just like when I promised to keep my spirits up if God would just show me; you know it. One more time, Gideon asks God for more proof. "Lord, I know I said I would not ask this this again, but I need that 337, just one more time." Been there; done that. I so feel Gideon's concerns. One more time he asks God for a sign with the fleece only this time, it would be for the fleece to be dry and the ground to be wet. Ah, a little harder test. How sneaky of Gideon. But, since we all know that nothing is too hard for God, Gideon woke the next morning to find things just as he had asked (Verses 39-40), again.

Chapters seven and eight go on to tell us the story of how God then reduced the number of Gideon's army from 30,000 to 300 warriors who proceeded to defeat every enemy they came up against. In the end, the children of Israel were freed, just as God had promised, and Gideon learned a new way to walk in faith.

Remember what we called this kind of faith? Blind faith. Again, we ask ourselves how many countless others were affected by Gideon's act of faith. We will never know, but we can be assured that the number is astounding. Once more, God chose one man to lead His people out of bondage. It was the Exodus all over again.

The story of Gideon is much more in depth and has many interesting highlights which we did not cover. When you take the time to study the book, you will be able to see a more vivid picture of his strength and faith. Maybe it is time for us to ask God what area of our lives need to be yielded to Him in blind faith. We may be surprised at what He shows us.

Lesson III – The Proving of Faith – Heb. 11:1 – Lord, You gave me grace.

Over the course of the last thirty years of my life, God has carried me through, and delivered me from, things that would lift the hearts and spirits of even the coldest and most callous of souls. I learned early in life to depend on Him to answer my specific prayers. I knew that I had to come before Him with a broken spirit (The sacrifices of God are a broken spirit – Ps. 51:17) and with clear petitions. I also knew that I had to kneel before Him in the closest state of righteousness I could achieve (The prayers of a righteous man accomplishes much – James 5:16). I had my usual daily quiet time where I would ask God for the generalities of life, but when faced with giants I knew could only be defeated by Him, I would find myself on my face before Him.

It is funny how that would always be my last recourse instead of my first. I could have saved myself a lot of pain and stress if I had inverted these two actions. Maybe I had to do it this way for dramatic effects, or maybe this was the way God intended it to be so that He would, as He should, receive the glory. I do not have the answers. What I do know is this. When we get on our face and ask Him in faith to deliver us, He always does. Always. I will come back to that later in this study and show you how I know, without question, this is true. As we continue from here, the next few characters will find themselves in many of the exact emotional situations where I have found myself. Likely, you will find that you have been there, as well.

Remember the spiraling effect I shared with you earlier? Because of the ongoing, seemingly forever growing, personal issues I faced, there were moments during the writing of this study when I thought I was not going to be able to continue. I thought I had prepared myself for the war I knew Satan would surely wage on my life, however, I would soon learn just how miserably I had failed. Maybe that was because I did not know how to prepare, or maybe I took for granted just how much I needed to prepare. Maybe I was overzealous in my urgency to get started. Maybe I thought I already had all the answers. Maybe, maybe, maybe, OR, just maybe it was supposed to happen this way. Maybe I would need another trip (I have lost count of how many I have made) into the Refiner's fire in order to clearly see the things God wanted me to point out and to have pointed out to me. Maybe God intended to use the battles as teaching tools to be sure I remembered why I was writing this. Maybe this was God's plan the entire time.

That's a long list of maybes to which we may never know the reasons. What I do know is that I shed more tears during the writing of this than I probably have over the last twenty years of my life. I also know that God always gets things done the way He intended for them to be done. His plan, though we may think differently, is not altered. The good news is that He *always* held me up. Now, I am not going to say there was not time lost wallowing in the pity pool, but when God had let me wallow long enough, He would come through with my 337 or some other rainbow to remind me that He was still in the midst of it all.

You have to wonder how we lose sight of that over and over again. Just like the children of Israel, God gets us out of the mess, we delve into another, and the vicious cycle starts again. In the last portion of this study, we are going to see the effects of what happens when we openly and honestly tell God that we know He is our only Hope, and when we walk in a type of faith that proves to be different than all the rest.

Have you ever come before God and told Him that if He did not choose to help you, there would be no way out? Again, I challenge you to revisit times in your life that can be compared to the next few characters we are going to look at. These people walked in **basic faith.** Interesting phrase, isn't it? So what exactly is basic faith? Basic faith is the kind of faith that simply assumes. It is the very essence of what faith is (Heb. 11:1.) Basic faith is the foundation of everything we believe and everything we hope for. If we could all achieve this in our lives, there would be no limit to the things God would give us. Ask God now to show you, through the next few pages, just how to accomplish that.

Mark 2 - If only we all had friends like these next examples. As we begin reading in Mark, we find that Jesus had come into the city of Capernaum. By this time in His ministry, word had spread about how He had healed countless people of the most dreadful diseases – even those that were known to only be cured by God. As was always the case, when the people heard He was nearby, they immediately ran to Him. While there were a variety of reasons people wanted to see Him, a very large focus at this time was on the healing powers He possessed. It seemed there was no end to what He could do, and all anyone had to do to receive a blessing was simply *believe*. However, this story takes a bit of a different twist.

As we begin our reading in Mark, the Bible tells us that as Jesus was reading the Scriptures, ". . . they came to Him bringing a paralytic who was carried by four men," (Mark 2:2). Now, let's get this into perspective. Jesus was in a house that was so packed with people wanting to hear Him teach, there was literally standing room only all the way to, and through, the doors and windows. As these mean neared the crowd, there was certainly commotion and even some assistance as they tried to get them inside to see Jesus. Notice "they came to Him bringing", and "carried by four men". As they worked to get through the crowd, realizing they could not get through, they decided to climb on top of the house and uncover a large section of the roof in order to lower the man down in front of Jesus. With great determination they fought the crowd, climbed the roof, lifted the man up, tore open a spot big enough to lower him through, then laid him in front of Jesus (Verse 4). These four men (who remain nameless) knew without question if they could just get their friend to Jesus, He would heal him.

How do we know this? Because as the story continues in verse five, the Bible tells us that Jesus ". . . saw their faith," and, as a result, said to the paralytic man, "Son, your sins are forgiven," (Mark 2:5). Stop right here and think about this for a long minute. This man asked Jesus for nothing. In fact, there is no indication as to whether or not he could even speak. The Scripture tells us that Jesus saw *their* (the paralytic man's friends) faith and because of *their* faith, He healed this man. These four nameless men had basic faith. In their hearts they knew, with *unwavering faith*, Jesus could and would heal their friend if *only* they believed. That is all it took.

Of course, as the story continues, Jesus eventually tells the man to get up and walk, and the man is completely healed (Verses 6-12). The entire scene played out as a witness to the huge crowd that had gathered and to the scribes who were in attendance.

Now, go back and revisit something. These four men certainly brought their friend to Jesus to be healed, but at this time in history, people equated certain illnesses and diseases with sin. If you were born with a particular handicap, it was assumed to be caused by the sin of your parents. If it came later in life, it was naturally a result of sin in your own life. I think it is interesting to point out that Jesus' first response was not "get up and walk," but *"Son, your sins are forgiven."* What was the reasoning behind this? Jesus was clearly making a statement about Who He was. It was common knowledge that no one had the power to forgive sin except God. So right there in front of the whole crowd, Jesus made Himself equal with God.

Let's make another side note here which will prove to be an important point. After Jesus said, "Your sins are forgiven," there was an immediate stirring in the crowd, particularly among the scribes. But notice the wording of the scripture. "And some of the scribes were sitting there reasoning in their hearts, 'Why does this Man speak blasphemies like this? Who can forgive sins but God alone,'" (Mark 2:6-7)? Look closely at the wording. They were reasoning *in their own hearts*.

The Bible does not say they started talking among themselves. Most of these men were intrigued by Jesus and were honestly seeking the truth, but being teachers in the church, this was more than they could bring themselves to imagine. So Jesus, knowing what they were thinking, asked them, "Why do you reason about these things in your hearts? Which is easier, to say to the paralytic 'Your sins are forgiven you', or to say, 'Arise, take up your bed and walk'? But that you may know that the Son of Man has the power on earth to forgive sins . . ." then looking to the paralytic man He said, "I say to you, arise, take up your bed, and go to your house," (Verses 6-11). Then comes the payoff in verse twelve. "Immediately, he arose, took up his bed, and went out in the presence of them all, so that all were amazed and glorified God saying, 'We never saw anything like this!'" (Mark 2:12). Notice that word *all*. It did not say all of the people except the scribes, or most of the people and some of the scribes. The word of God says *all*. God worked the situation so that He would get the glory, His will would be achieved, and people would come to believe.

How many hearts were changed that day, and how many have been changed since then because of the faith of those four unnamed men? We will never know the answer to that, but we can assume the domino effect began taking place and those men will receive credit for that in eternity. What if we could possess that kind of faith? How many lives would we receive credit for? Let that stay with you as we look to our next example.

Mark 5 – Talk about heart wrenching. As we read the stories in the Gospels, we find Jesus at work, and we see one miracle after another unfold. Many times, the situations seem hopeless, and we see people coming to Jesus as a last resort. That is just so us, isn't it? Remember as we said earlier, people do not change. So here in verses 21-24 of Mark 5, we see part one of a story about the faith of a father. The Bible tells us that Jesus had crossed over the river and was greeted by another "great multitude". As He began teaching, one of the rulers of the synagogue came to Him in desperation and told Him that his daughter was dying. He then told Jesus that if He (Jesus) would only come and see her, he *knew* that she would live.

Okay, let's gain a little perspective here. This man, Jarius, was a ruler in the synagogue which meant that he was a part of a group who was seeking to find Jesus guilty of blasphemy. The sentence for blasphemy was death. That meant he worked with men who were looking to find enough fault with Jesus to have Him put to death. Can you see how God was going to work in this situation?

Many times, God tries to get our attention and, when we refuse to give it to him, He uses a tragic event to get our attention. I am not saying God causes the tragedy, but He does use the circumstances. Think about the strength in that. God speaks and speaks and speaks, and when we just will not listen, something terrible happens. Then, what is our response? We hit our knees, or face, or bellies, and anything else that we think we need to hit in order to get God to hear us and before you know it, He has our undivided attention.

Such was the case with Jarius. As with most people, this tragedy sent him to the only Source of hope he believed was left. He went straight to Jesus and begged Him to save his child. So, this man no longer cared what his peers, family, or friends thought. He had one concern and that was for the life of his child. It is important to understand, though, at some point, this man had come to believe that Jesus was Who He said He was. How do we know this? Because he came to Jesus *in faith* and begged Him to spare his child's life. This man of Jewish faith, the leader of the church, had put his faith in Christ. Again, you wonder, how do we know this? Let's look at the Text. When you read earlier in the Bible (Mark 5:24), Jesus had started to leave with Jarius but he was delayed by the crowd. Then verses 35-43 tell us the beautiful story of faith.

As the ruler's friends came and told him that his daughter had died, before he could say a word, Jesus spoke to him and said, "Do not be afraid; only believe," (Verse 36). Obviously, that is exactly what Jarius did because as the story continues, Jesus goes on to the ruler's home and raises his daughter from death. Would He have done that had Jarius not followed Him in faith? Not likely. Chances are that had Jarius not believed, He would have taken a different attitude towards Jesus and likely blamed Him for his child's death. He certainly would not have welcomed Him into his house. In fact, as the crowd surely grumbled about Jesus' words, and they were undoubtedly angered by His attitude, had Jarius not believed, he would have gone home and prepared a funeral.

So what do we see? The father and Jewish leader lived out his basic faith and, as a result, his child was not only healed, but raised from death. The Bible does not tell us what happened at Jarius' home after that, but let's use a little inference. Back in verses 38-40 of Mark, we read that when Jesus arrived, He found a group of people who "wept and wailed loudly," (Verse 38). Jesus walked in and very calmly said, "Why make this commotion and weep? This child is not dead, but sleeping." What happened next is where we find our message. When Jesus said that, the crowd started laughing and ridiculing Him, so He had them put outside while He proceeded to where the little girl was (Verse 40). As you could imagine, I am sure these people were standing in front of the house creating a stir because Jesus had made them leave. The only ones allowed in were Jarius and his wife, Peter, James and John.

Imagine, if you will, what happened to that crowd of angry people when they found out that this little girl was alive and well. It does not take much to figure out what their reaction was. The anger and complaining would have quickly been replaced with amazement and disbelief. Now, they would be put in a position to have to choose to either accept Who Jesus was or to reject Him. There is no account of how many believed on that day, but given the magnitude of the miracle, as well as whose home it had taken place in, it would be right to assume there were quite a few new believers.

On that day, because of Jarius' faith, we can assume his wife and anyone in his household likely came to believe Who Jesus was. What an amazing story. What an emotional story. I wonder what would happen if in our darkest hours, we found the strength to walk in that kind of basic faith. Put yourself in that position and ask if you would have what it took to stand firm and believe.

As we were reading through this Text, we passed over one of the most famous stories of faith of all time, the story of the woman with "the issue of blood". Remember her? She was actually part of the crowd that detained Jesus while He was on His way to Jarius' house. The Bible tells us her story in verses 25-34. Studies have concluded that this woman who had the "issue" had actually been dealing with it for twelve years. Twelve long, frustrating years. She had done everything she could possibly think of in order to find some kind of relief. She had seen so many doctors that she had actually run out of money. On top of that, after all her money was spent, she was still sick. Like Jarius, she had come on that day in desperation to Jesus, however, she was unable to come face to face with Him.

Now get the picture. Jesus had crossed the river and been met by a large crowd which the Bible refers to as a "great multitude". This woman was part of the crowd. Jesus stepped out of the boat and was immediately surrounded by people calling out and begging Him for help. She, like everyone else, was just trying to get to Him. Suddenly, Jarius appeared and was allowed to get through because of his position in the church. He told Jesus his story, but as Jesus started to go with him, He was pressed by others who had been trying to get help. As He was moving through the crowd, the woman spoke only to herself, "If I could *just touch His clothes*, I would be made well," (Verse 28). There seems to be a trend with these statements of faith, doesn't there? Obviously, these were not just words people were saying to each other to gain popularity. The woman was speaking to herself, kind of like when we think out loud. It just happens that her thought was, "If I could just touch His clothes."

She fought her way through the multitude and managed to grab a piece of Jesus' robe as He passed by. Immediately, she was made well. Notice that word *immediately*. That is what the Bible tells us in verse 29. She did not have to wait any time at all. She had believed with absolute certainty in her heart that Jesus could heal her, and she had trusted that He would. Then, notice Jesus' response. He stopped and turned around, looking at the huge number of people and asked, "Who touched Me," (Verse 30)? Very interesting when you consider that thousands of people were surrounding him.

Of course, Jesus knew the answer to this already, but like all the other times, this was an opportunity to make God's power known. At this point, the woman was filled with fear, but she fell at Jesus' feet and told Him that it had been her who had done this. Notice Jesus' exact words of response. "Daughter, your *faith* has made you well. Go in peace, and be healed of your affliction," (Mark 5:34).

Remember the commotion that happened when Jesus told the paralytic man to get up and walk? I can imagine the same type of reaction was probably taking place here, however there was not much time for response, because the Bible tells us that while He was still speaking, Jarius' servants came to deliver bad news to him. In the meantime, though, He had left the crowd to marvel at both the immediate healing and the statement He had just made about faith and being made well.

I cannot point out enough that in each situation, Jesus wanted God to receive the glory. Had this not been the case, He could have just continued on and let the woman go quietly on her way. However, because of His response, I expect there were many people who questioned her as to what had happened and, as a result, came to believe Who Jesus was.

Before we go on to the next story, I want to take a little journey into what happens when God is faced with unbelief. As Jesus carried out His public ministry, people flocked to Him for one of two reasons. They either wanted to receive a miracle, or they wanted to witness a miracle. Everyone was curious as to Who He was and how He was able to do the things He did. Within these groups of people, however, there was another division: Those who wanted to believe Jesus was Who He said He was and those who wanted to prove that He was a false prophet.

Staying in Mark, we see as we begin to read in chapter 6 that as Jesus left from Jarius' home, He took His disciples and went to His own country. At this point in His ministry, many had come to accept and believe Who He was because of His teachings and the miracles He continuously performed. However, things would be different as He came before the people of His home town.

Let's remember something as we look at the next few verses. These were people Jesus had lived alongside, played with when He was a child, grown up with, and worked with. They were all neighbors who knew each other very well and knew what was going on in each other's lives. Certainly, they had all heard about the things Jesus was doing in the surrounding regions. By now, word had spread everywhere that He was a great teacher, healer, and all around miracle man, and He had become quite popular throughout that land. So once He came into His home town and the Sabbath came, the Bible tells us that Jesus "began teaching in the synagogue". (Mark 6:2) But notice the crowd's reaction to this Man Who had been so widely accepted in so many other towns. "And many hearing Him were *astonished* saying, 'Where did this Man get these things? And what wisdom is this which is given to Him, that such mighty works are performed by his hands! Is this not the carpenter, the Son of Mary, and brother of James, Joseph, Judas and Simon? And are not His sisters here with us?' So they were offended at Him." (Mark 6:2-3) To put it into words we use today, these people were *blown away* by the audacity that He would come there proclaiming to be something special. After all, they all knew where He was from, so who did He think He was fooling? They did not know where He got the power to do the things He did, but they knew this one thing for sure. He was no one special, and He was not going to get anything over on them. They would show Him.

What a sad story. Because of their unbelief, souls were lost. In verse 4, Jesus addressed their unbelief. "A prophet is not without honor *except* in his own country, among his own relatives, and in his own house." Just look at the heartbreaking reality of what happened. "Now He could do no *mighty* work there, except that He laid His hands on a *few* sick people and healed them, and He marveled because of their unbelief. Then He went about the villages in a circuit, teaching." (Mark 6:5-6) It is safe to say this story, and the lesson intended, speaks well for itself. I pray that none of us miss out on the blessings God wants to bring into our lives because of a lack of faith.

John 11 – In this last example, I want to look at the hearts of the characters. This is the story of Lazarus. We see in this story the epitome of faith, hopelessness, despair, brokenness, victory and elation. We have all experienced, and will again experience, each of these emotions in our lifetime. As much as we dread most of these moments, the Bible tells us these are the times when God is closest to us. (Ps. 34:18)

As John opens, the story immediately begins by saying that Lazarus had become sick. Remember, the family of Lazarus was very close to Jesus. Notice in verse three that the sisters of Lazarus (Martha and Mary) sent word to Jesus letting Him know, but look how they worded it, "Lord, behold, he whom You love is sick." Now, does that imply that the Lord did not love everyone? Of course not. We all know that God loves all of us equally. However, Jesus did have a close personal relationship with Mary, Martha and Lazarus, and it would be safe to say they were much like family, as is pointed out in verse 5. Given the close ties, the story offers a little more emotion. The Bible does not tell us what was wrong with Lazarus, but whatever was going on, his sisters felt the need to let Jesus know, indicating that it was something serious. But look back to verse 4 and notice the calming words of Christ as He said, "This sickness is not unto death, *but for the glory of God, that the Son of God may also be glorified through it."* Jesus very explicitly said to the sisters, *through the ones who had brought Him the message that* Lazarus was not going to die from this. He even went on and told them why this was happening.

Notice here, though, that this message had been *sent* to Jesus. Remember, He was teaching, and everywhere He went, a huge crowd always followed Him. So, when these messengers arrived, everyone around heard Jesus' response. Can you see the story being set up?

Let's get the big picture. Mary knows without question that Jesus is the Christ. She is the one who anointed His feet with her tears and dried them with her hair. That was a beautiful story of redemption. (Luke 7:36-39) Now she fears her brother is going to die and, relying on basic faith, sends for help from the Only One she knows can save him. Therefore, I am sure when the words came from Jesus telling her it was going to be okay, she had complete confidence that it would be.

Of course, the story had to take a dramatic turn. Remember, Jesus had said God was going to receive the glory here, so there had to be more to it. In verse 6, we see that Jesus purposely stayed two days longer, then began to make the journey back to Judea. Look at all the important factors. The sisters sent for Jesus in desperation. He told them, *through the messengers*, Lazarus would not die from this sickness. He made the statement that this would be for the glory of God, and the Son of God would be glorified. Then, He continued about His business as though nothing was wrong. But, look at what happened next. Jesus told His disciples they were going to Judea, a place where they had tried to put Him to death. When the disciples protested, Jesus spoke to them and told them that darkness was about to be turned to light, and eyes would finally be opened.

You would think by now that these men who walked with Jesus daily would get it. Verses 11-15 paint a clear picture of exactly what I am pointing out. Jesus started by telling his disciples that they had to go to Judea, in spite of the danger, because Lazarus was sleeping and He had to wake Him. Puzzled, they responded by saying, "Well, Lord, if he is sleeping, he will wake up." (John 11:12) Basically, "Jesus, we don't need to go there and risk our lives to wake him up from sleep. What are You thinking?" Here is a better question. What were *they* thinking? Jesus had just said He would be glorified through this. Where was their faith? You would think of all the people in the world, these men would have more than anyone else. However, it seems like over and over they displayed just the opposite.

So, look at Jesus' response to them and the exact wording in verses 14-15. It almost makes you want to laugh out loud. "Then Jesus said to them *plainly*, 'Lazarus is dead, and I am glad *for your sakes that I was not there that you may believe.* Nevertheless, let's go to him.'" (John 11:14-15) Can you imagine the moment of silence and what had to be going through their minds? He just told them Lazarus was sleeping and He had to go wake him. Now, He was saying in plain words that Lazarus was dead, and He was glad.

If you think for one moment these men were standing solidly in their faith, you may want to rethink it. Remember, these are men who Jesus continually had to prove Himself to and, as the Bible tells us, would continue to have to prove Himself to. But, you have to love Thomas' response. "Then, Thomas, who is called the Twin, said to his fellow disciples, 'Well then, let's go too, so that we can all die with Him.'" (John 11:16) Call that faith, love, or a little of both. I believe Thomas made this statement in faith believing that God would be glorified just as Jesus had said, and if that meant death, then so be it.

So, they all left and made their way to Judea. When they arrived, Lazarus had already been in the tomb for four days. The Bible tells us that many had come to comfort the two sisters and they were all still there at the house. I expect that many of them who were there were likely part of the crowd who had heard Jesus say that Lazarus' sickness was "not unto death". Certainly, the messengers were there. When Martha heard that Jesus was there, she ran out to greet Him, but Mary stayed inside.

Notice carefully the conversation that took place next between Martha and Jesus, beginning with verse 21. "Now, Martha said to Jesus, 'Lord, if You had been here, my brother would not have died.'" Pay close attention to her next words. "But *even now* I know whatever You ask of God, God will give You." I am not sure Martha realized exactly what she was asking and hoping for, but in her heart, she knew that Jesus was able to do anything. Look at the words closely. "If You had been here . . . But even now." I think there is no question this is a clear cut statement of basic faith. "Lord, this terrible thing has happened, but You can fix it." Isn't that what she was saying to Him? Let's look on.

Jesus responded to her and said, "Your brother will rise again." But in verse 24 she tells Jesus she knows Lazarus will rise again in the last day. So, if you are asking, "How can she say to Jesus she knows He can change things," then turn around and say, "Well, I hear You, but . . .?" It is simple. We do this all the time. These are blanket statements we make when something seems too good to be true.

As the story continues, Jesus poses a question in verses 24-25. First He tells her, "I am the Resurrection and the Life. He who believes in Me, though he may die, he shall live. And whoever lives and believes in Me shall never die." Then He asks her, "Do you believe this?" Now comes the beautiful confession of faith in Christ. She said to Him, "Yes, Lord, I **believe that You are the Christ, the Son of God, Who is come into the world**." (John 11:27) That was the deal clincher for her. She knew what she was asking and what she was confessing. She could only now hope for what she knew was impossible for anyone other than God.

At that point, Martha went to tell her sister that Jesus was looking for her. As Mary got up and ran out the door, the people who were there with her followed, assuming she was going to the tomb to weep. Can you see God working here? Remember, the whole idea is for God to be glorified. Jesus' had said that when the story began. Jesus sent for her knowing the crowd would follow here, then there would be a captive audience for the events that would soon take place.

Notice as Mary reached Jesus, she fell to the ground at His feet and said, "Lord, if You had been here, my brother would not have died." (Verse 32) Try to imagine the flood of emotions she was feeling. Here she was at Jesus' feet, confessing that she knew He could have saved her brother, yet He chose not to. However, she *still* fell at His feet, just as she had done when she had washed his feet with her tears. As she lay there weeping, her heart feeling like it was being ripped from her body, Jesus seeing her tears and those of the ones with her, became troubled in His Spirit. He asked where they had laid Lazarus and the people proceeded to show Him. That Bible tells us that then, in His humanity, Jesus wept. (John 11:35)

That needs a moment of reflection. Jesus, moved to compassion, wept for their broken hearts. Now, you may ask yourself why He would cry for them when He knew what was about to happen. The answer is simple. Remember, Jesus was flesh and blood with emotions, just like us. What is our response when we see someone hurting? Most, if not all of us, will become troubled and, if they are really upset, many of us will cry with them. That is just human nature. So, this is what Jesus was experiencing. He was also showing the Jews that He did care about people. I also believe that Jesus was moved at the godly love Mary displayed for Him even though she believed He had allowed her brother to die. I cannot think of any other story that shows this magnitude of faith and love?

Then, we see the moment of triumph. Remember, "So that God will get the glory and the Son of God will be glorified." (Verse 4) As the Jews mumbled among themselves about how much Jesus loved Lazarus and why He had not saved him (verses 36-37), Jesus again became troubled and proceeded to the tomb and told them to take the stone away. In astonishment, Martha objected telling Jesus that there would surely be a stench since Lazarus had been dead for four days. But, look at the awesome words of God here in verse 40. "Did I not say to you that **IF** you would believe, you would see the glory of God?" Then, there is silence. Martha experienced a few thoughtful silent moments with God that reminded her she had to step out in faith based on the words she had just confessed.

Remember, only a few moments before she had said, "I know You can do anything." The Bible does not tells us this, but I am sure after that moment of silence, Martha stepped back and allowed those men to remove the stone. I can just see her looking into Jesus' eyes as she backed away, almost seemingly hypnotized, her face filled with fear, uncertainty and resignation. Then Jesus looked toward heaven and said, "Father, I thank You that You have heard Me. And I know that You always hear Me, but *because of the people who are standing by I said this, that they may believe that You sent Me.*" (Verse 41-42) Then Jesus cried out at the open tomb, "Lazarus, come forth!", and in that glorious moment the Bible says, "He who had died came out, bound hand and foot with grave clothes, and his face was wrapped with a cloth." (Verse 44) And Jesus said, "Loose him, and let him go."

What I would give to have been part of the crowd on that incredible day. I cannot even imagine for a second the range of emotions that swept every single person there. Martha, having stepped out in faith, had received a miracle the likes of which most of us will never come close to receiving. Mary, having cried out for help in adoration and confession, had received a place in the Lord's heart we can all only pray we will have the faith to achieve. The Jews, questioning and looking for a miraculous sign, had witnessed a resurrection the likes of which no one had ever seen, thereby receiving the answers they had long been seeking. But most importantly, God had received the glory, and Jesus was glorified just as He had promised.

What a story. What an incredibly, amazing, life altering story. Here is a challenge. If you ever find yourself wondering (and you surely will) if God really cares about how you feel or what you want, go back to this story of faith and victory and you will have your answer. Basic faith. That is what it took. That is all it took. Do you have that in your life?

Conclusion

The phone rang at 2 a.m., and a familiar voice choking back tears on the other end softly said, "Momma, how do you know what your 337 is?" It was my baby boy who had been one of many who helped me along as I took this journey in faith. "Josh," I said, "That's for you to decide. I can't tell you what it is, but it doesn't

matter. I found mine by coming before God over and over again seeking His guidance. Whatever you choose, just lay it before God and trust Him to use that as your sign, your promise, your rainbow, your 337."
"I'm struggling with some stuff, Momma," he says. "I know, but you know what else? God already knows," I answered, "and this is an opportunity for you. Just get before Him and lay it all out. He'll know what to do and if you let Him, He will guide you through it all."
"Thanks, I will. I love you, Mom. Goodnight," he whispered. "Goodnight, Josh. I love you, too," I said. I hung up the phone and smiled at the idea that I had been able to be a picture of faith for him during the previous months.

As I laid there in the dark, I thought about how God had been so good to me over the past few months and about all the people I had told about my 337. I let my mind ponder their different responses and about how I had finally been convinced to lay out a deadline for God to let me hear from this man. Now, the deadline was very near. I had told God that if nothing changed by the first week of the New Year, I was going to assume I had misunderstood something and move on with my life. A panic almost came over me as I thought about how that seemed to be putting God to the test. I cried and begged His forgiveness and told Him again that it was not my lack of faith in Him, but in myself. Once again, I was right back in that pit. How did I keep ending up there? Then, in the whisper of the moment, I began remembering all the times He had shown me my rainbow, and how it would come. I thought about the day I was sitting at the traffic light and, in tears, told God that I needed to see it in a way that He had not shown it to me before. Two seconds later, the light for the cross traffic changed and there, crossing right in front of me, was a white van with 337 in big, black numbers on the side. I cried and thanked Him and promised not to ask again. How funny is that? I am just like Gideon. Four days later I was driving down the road again begging God for my sign one more time. Just one more last time, God. I promise. Uh, huh. Just then, I looked over and there on the side of the road, of all places, was a giant digital clock with bold red numbers that said 337. "Thank you, God, I will not ask for it again. Thank You, thank You, thank You," I cried. About four miles down the road, I happened to look at the clock in my car. It read 3:34 and I realized, the clock with the 337 was off by several minutes. I was awed again. A few days later, I was at home watching a movie, feeling that familiar panic but afraid to ask God for anything. Remember, I had promised, again, so I dared not ask. But my spirit must have been praying for me because as I felt myself spiraling, I noticed the main character in the movie, who happened to be Tom Hanks, holding a piece of paper in his hand. The paper had a number written on it. Guess what the number was? How in the world could I ever doubt? If anyone was going to find a way, it would be me. I prayed myself to sleep holding onto the hope God had given me. A few days later, I was driving home from work. It was New Year's Eve, a day for celebration. It was cold, dreary, and raining and time was ticking away. As I realized the position I had taken and that this was the end of the year, I cried out to God in my panic stricken voice and begged Him, yet again, to please, please, please show me my 337. I told Him I was weak, and desperate, and scared. I told Him things about myself that, of course, He already knew but I felt had to be confessed. I told Him that I needed this now more than ever. I could barely breathe because I was crying so hard. Then, through my tears, the blur from the rain, and the traffic, there it was. On the front of a building as part of the address. How awesome is that? How awesome is God? I wonder if He was weeping with me. I do not know, but what I do know is that He was there with me, just as His word promised. I thanked Him again, as always, and allowed His presence to console me. Two days later, I signed onto my computer and there saw the message I had been praying and waiting for all that time. "We need to talk. Send me your number. I will call you tomorrow." I did not cry. I did not smile. I did not leap for joy. I simply sent the number, went in the other room, lit the fire, and laid on the couch. As I softly thanked God for His faithfulness, He said, "It's time to write the Bible study."

Though I wish I could say I followed in obedience and wrote this book, sadly that is not the case. Because God loves me, He fulfilled His promise and gave me what I had asked for. However, in my excitement, I forgot about what I had promised God. That would be the event that led me to the silent moment I shared at the beginning of this study. Of course, I blamed God for my mistakes. However, on that day when He pointed out to me that I failed to do what He had called me to do, I repented, wrote this book, and did not look back. Though He could have chosen to break me, My Loving Heavenly Father, instead, blessed my life again.

I wonder what it's going to take for us to get it. How many more miracles are we going to have to read about or witness? How many more prayers are we going to have to see answered? How many more disasters are we going to have to survive? Will there ever be an end? Based on history, the answer seems to be an infinite number. It is like we get it, but then when we are faced with an upheaval, we lose it. Then we get it again only to lose it on another upheaval. This has been true since the beginning of creation. We have read only a few of the stories recorded, and there are countless more in the Bible. Aside from that, there are many, many more that were never written about. The story line is always the same, though. That is how we end up defeated and become victims of the world. I do not know about you, but I do not want to be like that. I challenge you right now, in this very moment, to get on your face before God, lay your life at His feet, and step out into a journey of faith that will take you to a new height in your relationship with Him. Find your 337 and trust Him with it. If you do not need it now, trust me, you will need it in the future. When the trials and struggles come in life, will you have what it takes to walk through that fire and come out the other side with renewed confidence and boldness? Time will tell. It is a question of faith.

God Bless.

Update

Since the writing of this book, there have been a couple of updates that are important. These not only left me in awe, but also gave me more experiences that I felt needed to be shared.

Josh's Story

I had told Josh to choose his sign, and to trust God in whatever happened. He was praying over a situation that had him so distraught, and he knew that he had lost all control.

After he prayed and left it with God, he walked into his office at work the next day and saw, of all things, a bottle of wine sitting on the desk. This was strange for several reasons. Though he worked in a restaurant which did offer wine, no one was allowed to take a bottle, empty or full, anywhere in the administrative parts of the restaurant. To do so could cost the restaurant its license. He had also served many glasses and bottles of wine during his years as a restaurant employee, and he had never seen or heard of this particular wine.

He took the bottle and asked each of the employees if they knew anything about it, but no one had ever seen or heard of this wine, and no one confessed to bringing it into the restaurant. He checked the wine list to see the names they offered, and the name of this wine was not on the list.

Perplexed, shaken, amazed, and in awe, he went back to his office and picked up the phone to call me. I will never forget that call. "Mom," he said, his voice trembling. "Josh, what's wrong," I cried out, fearing he was in trouble. "After we got off the phone, I prayed like I have never prayed before," He said. "I asked God to take everything out of my life that kept me from Him. I begged for His forgiveness, and I asked for His guidance. I begged Him for a sign. I asked Him for my 337."

By now, he was crying, and I knew something big was coming. "Mom," he said through his tears. "Yes, Josh. What is it?" I asked. "He answered me. When I walked into my office at work, there on the desk was a bottle of wine. It was black with big red numbers. Guess what the number were, Mom." I still cry when I remember this moment. The name of the wine is Noble Vines 337 Cabernet Sauvignon, and no one in the restaurant ever figured out where it came from.

Josh cried out in faith, and trusted his answer. He has never looked back, and God has blessed him beyond measure.

Kip's Story

Remember how I had ended the original book? Kip had left me a message on the computer, and I had sent him my phone number. Well, the next morning, he called me while I was away from my phone. When I returned, I saw a message on the screen . . . Missed Call – Kip. I was really upset that I had missed his call, but he did leave me a voicemail, which I found interesting, because he never leaves voicemail for anyone, even now. As I played it back, he explained that he was going to work, and he asked me to call him at 3:30 or 4:00 that afternoon.

I was so excited! I could barely get through the day. At 3:30, I called him back, but I got a message that said the number was disconnected. What!?! I tried it again and again, all with the same result. I was perplexed and upset, and I didn't know what to think. After a few hours going around and around in my mind and with God, I finally went to bed. I was exhausted. The last time I look at the clock before I fell asleep, it said it was 2:17.

When my alarm went off the next morning, I had a hard time getting up. I kept hearing it go off but in my mind, I couldn't figure out the sound. Finally, I got up and looked at my phone. It was 5:48, and there on the screen it said I had a missed call. I looked at the details, and there it was again . . . Missed call – Kip. He had called at around 4 a.m., and he left another message.

What was going on? He said in the message that he didn't know why I hadn't called back, and he asked me again to call him back at around the same time. So, that afternoon, I tried again with the same results. It was so strange. I was absolutely in panic mode, so I got on the computer as soon as I got home and sent him a message asking him to call me.

Within a few minutes, my phone rang and there on the screen it said – Kip calling. We talked for a few minutes about how each other had been, and we caught up on what was going on with our families and our lives. He told me how much he had missed me and how he wanted to work things out, but he didn't understand why I had not called him back. When I told him what had been happening, he asked me what number I had been calling. I told him it was his number on my phone. He explained that he had changed his number a few months back, and it didn't make sense that his new number didn't come up on my phone. Of course, it didn't make sense. Why would it?

We hung up to check out the number. I called him from my contacts with his name, and it said the number was not working. When he called me back, it said, Kip calling. When I called the new number he had given me, it was not listed in my contacts, but he answered the phone.

Once we were together, we went to the phone company and asked them how that was possible. Their response . . . we have no idea. That is actually not possible.

Stories of Discouragement

Most times when I have shared this story, people are awed. They wonder if these things really happened, and they ask how I can explain it. Some take it by faith, others just dismiss the events, but others actually question what happened. In fact, numerous people told me that I could pick any number, and that if I looked for it long enough, I would finally see it. So, this is for the doubters.

While we were not yet together, I was seeking clarity because, as you would guess, I was a little shaken by the negative responses. During that time, I was doing some recording with one of my friends, and I had to meet him at the studio in Franklin, Tennessee.

On the drive from Georgia, I prayed again, confessing my fears, and I asked God to help me again. I told Him that if he would show me something different, I would confront those that had caused me to doubt and, no matter how bad things ever became again, I would not drift away from my belief in the message I was receiving. I would finally know, even when someone might be telling me differently, things would be okay from that moment.

The new sign I asked for was 33768. Of course, it has significance to no one but me, but I knew what it meant. Once I got to the hotel and settled in for the night, I was flipping through the TV while talking on the phone. When my phone call took a serious turn, I laid down the remote and focused only on the call.

When the call was over, I looked at the TV screen. It was black and had no picture. There in the corner were the numbers I had asked, 3 3 7 6 8. Each number, though, was in a corner making the shape of a square with one number in the middle, so that was not clear enough for me. At that point, I said out loud, "God, that is not good enough. I have to see them in order." Yep. That is exactly the way I said it. When would I get it?

The next day, we finished the recording, and I decided to head home, because bad weather was coming. I had been home only a couple of hours and was working on the computer, when things started to get really dark. The tornado siren went off, and the TV started beeping. On the bottom of the screen was a message that said, "The National Weather Service in Peachtree City has Issued a Tornado Warning for Gwinnett County. Message numbers 33764, 33765, 33766, 33767." I was watching the numbers go up and wondering what was about to happen. Suddenly, the message just stopped. I got up and looked around, watched the radar, and realized it was not going to be near where I was. The siren stopped, and the sky cleared a little. Though I thought the message and the events were strange, I went back to my work on the computer.

No sooner had I sat down, the TV started beeping again. There, across the bottom of the screen, was this message . . . 33768 . . . 33768 . . . 33768 . . . 33768 . . . 33768. That was it. Nothing else. In that moment, all I could do was stare.

What an incredible moment. What an incredible story. Most importantly, what an incredible God.

There are no other updates, and there will be none. God has answered, and that is all that matters. From this point on, it's A Question of Faith.

Notes

Notes

I would like to give a special thanks to my children, who supported me though this entire journey. They have loved me, helped me, and believed in me, far more than I deserve.

I also want to give a special thanks to Amy Strickland. In some of my darkest moments, she was there listening, encouraging, and praying for me as I sought God's will.

Made in the USA
Columbia, SC
06 August 2025